LOVE, SLEEP & DREAMS

Stanislaus Eric Stenbock (1860–1895), Count of Bogesund, was born in the South West England to Lucy Sophia Frerichs, an English cotton heiress, and Count Erich Stenbock, who was of a distinguished Swedish family of the Baltic German House of nobility in Reval. He inherited his family's estates in 1885 and returned to live in his manor house at Kolkbriefly for a period before returning to England. In his life he published three volumes of poetry, *Love, Sleep & Dreams*, *Myrtle, Rue and Cypress*, and *The Shadow of Death*, as well as one collection of short stories, *Studies of Death*. He died as a result of alcoholism and opium addiction.

ERIC, COUNT STENBOCK

LOVE, SLEEP & DREAMS
A VOLUME OF VERSE

THIS IS A SNUGGLY BOOK

This edition Copyright © 2019
by Snuggly Books.
All rights reserved.

ISBN: 978-1-943813-89-6

This Snuggly Books edition is an unabridged version of that which was published by A. Thomas Shrimpton & Son; Simpkin Marshall & Co, in 1881.

Contents

Εἰς τὸν ἐρώμενον / *11*
The Ballad of the Dead Sea Fruit / *27*
Song / *31*
Song / *35*
The Song of the Unwept Tear / *39*
Ode to the East Sea / *43*
Cradle Song / *47*
Child Grief / *51*
The Two Sleepers and One that Watcheth / *55*
Παιδικά / *59*
Ζιζάνια / *63*
All Souls' Day / *67*
Sapphics / *71*
Translations from Heine / *75*
"Ganymede" from Goethe / *83*
Dedication / *87*

LOVE, SLEEP & DREAMS

Εἰς τὸν ἐρώμενον.

or,

A Decade of Sighs
on a Lost Love

Prelude

I HAD a vision of Love crucified—
Love crucified in feet, in hands, and heart;
I looked on the pierced side of Love,
I saw a wound upon the heart of Love,
From which flowed blood and roses:—
Wounded hast thou mine heart, my love, mine
        own;
Seest thou my life-blood trickling drop by drop,
Till the last vital drop hath flowed therefrom?—
But with my blood there are commingled roses—
    For are not these my songs? as roses
    Let them be planted on my grave.

I.

I TRY to sing of other things,
    But I only sing of thee;
For I only think of thee, my love:—
    Wert thou not all to me?

What shall this broken lyre play,
    But the same old melody?—
That melody of thee, my love;
    Wert thou not all to me?

For what have I in heaven above,
    Or on the earth but thee?
And what is life itself, my love,
    Wert thou not all to me?

II.

COULD'ST thou not watch with me
    One single hour?
Could'st thou not give to me
    One single flower?

Others have other loves,
    Can'st thou love me?
Out of a thousand loves
    Have I chosen thee.

Mine own, my one ewe lamb
    Will they take from me?
Have they not many sheep?
    I have but thee.

III.

IT is for thee too slight for tears,
    That same, that bitter grief;
Which is for me too deep for tears,
    For respite, or relief.

For thee 'tis very light to bear,
    That same, that galling pain,
Which wastes mine inmost soul away,
    And sears my heart in twain.

IV.

NO! I will not complain,
    Though my heart be rent in twain;
Though my spirit be stricken sore,
    Yet I will not complain.

Thy wondrous smile, thy voice,
    Thy least step on the stair;
Each movement of thy graceful form,
    The perfume of thine hair—

These are to me so dear, so dear,
    And give me so much pain,
I find it difficult to say
    That I will not complain.

V.

EACH tear is as an arrow,
    It penetrates so deep
Into my heart; how dreadful
    It is to see thee weep!

Thy tears are shed so lightly,
    Thy tears are not for me,
Yet when I see thee weeping,
    I almost weep for thee.

I am to thee as nothing,
    I am so little dear,
I am not worth the priceless
    Price of a single tear.

VI.

I CANNOT look upon that face,
    From which beams a light divine;
I am distracted by the grace
    Of those slender limbs of thine.

By the strange music of thy laugh
    My spirit to the depths is shattered;
I long the passing breath to quaff
    From every word thy lips have uttered.

Thy tears are poison, and thy laugh
    Is fiendish, infinite derision;
Thy words are knives that cut in half
    The remnant of our souls' division.

I cast my pearls before the swine,
    I have no weapon to defend me;
My heart, my life, my soul were thine,
    And can'st thou turn again and rend me?

VII.

THAT pain—that galling pain,
   That rends the heart in twain;
Oh, that intolerable pain!
   That pain which is above
     All pains, that pain of broken love;
That pain of love self-slain;
To love and not be loved again!

Deserted—forsaken—alone,
My love, my all, mine own,
For me the world is made desolate;
Ever wailing I wait,
At the threshold of the gate.

There are many fairer by far than you,
   There are fairer women, and youths more fair,
   With bright, soft eyes, and curious hair,

But I found them all less fair than you:—
And you—what do you care?

The bitter cup you gave to me,
    Unto the dregs I quaff,
    And you stand by and laugh:
And all men laugh too, seeing me;
    You laugh, all laugh, I laugh,
Whilst from my heart a secret flood
Flows on for ever, of tears, of blood.

VIII.

DARLING, I know you never understood
    That vain, that blind, that passionate desire:
Ah! I was mad to think you ever could,
    Yet is my soul burnt up with torturing fire.

Live on, love on, enjoy and see the light,
    Think not on me, nor on my love; but I
Am weary of the life you once made bright,
    So very weary, that I fain would die.

IX.

AH, then! when my heart was breaking,
    The look of mine eyes was sad:
But now that my heart is broken,
    My aspect is almost glad.

Yet my heart is broken, broken,
    Our love is for ever fled;
Each tie that bound us is severed,
    Life of my life is dead.

X.

I BEGGED at thy door for bread,
    And thou gavest me a stone;
Thou turnedst away thine head,
    And did'st leave me standing alone.

I begged at thy door for meat,
    And thou gavest me a snake;
Thou gavest me poison to eat,
    And gall my thirst to slake.

Finale

THE fallen petals of the rose,
    The fallen feathers of the dove,
And the time of swiftly-falling snows,
    Are strewn on the tomb of Love.

A shroud of soft and silent snows
    Covers his body—he is dead:
The fallen petals of the rose,
    Are strewn about his head.

And yet Love died before the rose,
    Long ere the snows began to fall;
And now, the soft white silent snows
    Become his funeral pall.

The Ballad
of the Dead Sea Fruit

WHERE lie buried the ruins of Sodom,
    In the depths of the dead salt sea,
On the banks of the Dead Sea waters,
    There groweth a wondrous tree;

Well waxen with leaves and branches,
    But canker lies at the root,
And thereon are strange fair apples,
    And this is the "Dead Sea fruit."

Whoso shall eat of these apples,
    Which appear so fair and sweet,
In his mouth they shall turn to ashes;
    Ah! woe to him that shall eat.

Yea, woe to him that touches
    E'en this forbidden fruit,

Of the tree so fair and goodly,
    But with canker at the root.

Ask not, if thou know'st not already,
    What manner of tree this be
Which grows on the ruins of Sodom,
    On the banks of the dead salt sea.

Song

"Quoniam dederit delectis suis somnum."

HE giveth sleep to His belovèd,
  Sweetest of all things, sleep;
But I am not of His belovèd,
  Therefore I cannot sleep.

He giveth tears to His belovèd,
  And His beloved weep;
But I am not of His belovèd,
  Therefore I cannot weep.

Song

I SEE thee toil long weary hours,
    Wandering and searching through the snow:
What seekest thou? I seek for flowers,
    But I find none—ah! woe.

In my father's garden are many roses,
    All sorts of roses, red and white;
The honeysuckle climbs and closes,
    Straining to reach the light.

The Song of the Unwept Tear

I DREAMED a dreadful dream, almost
    Too terrible to tell;
I dreamed that you and I, my love,
    Together were in Hell.

I dreamed in all eternity
    We two together were;
Condemned each other's face and limbs
    In hate and rage to tear.

I dreamed your kisses keen, my love,
    Bit my flesh through and through;
I tasted the salt taste of blood,
    My love, as I kissed you.

I dreamed your soft warm limbs, my love,
    Burnt with Hell's furious fire;

And demons laughed, and said, This is
    The end of your desire.

Think'st thou they weep with many tears,
    Deem'st thou their brows are knit with pain?
Ah no! far worse than that, they laugh—
    Their laugh is hollow and insane.

Almost too horrible to hear,
    Too terrible to tell,
The song about the unwept tear,
    And the laughter heard in Hell.

Ode to the East Sea

MY heart is pierced, my spirit breaketh,
    My tears are salter than thy brine,
My soul with broken passion acheth,
    Take me to thee, O Mother mine.

"Poor stricken soul, what dost thou weeping?
    Are thou then weary of thy life?
Would'st thou be as the dead that, sleeping,
    Have passed from passion, pain and strife?"

Would that I could dissolve in tears,
    If tears were given me to weep.
Have I not lived these many years—
    And all that I long for now is sleep?

My life is blank, and dark, and dreary,
    Undone is all that I desired,

Kiss me, for I am very weary,
    Lay me to sleep, for I am tired.

'Tis a soft bed, a feathery pillow,
    Oh, let me rest upon thy wave;
Lull me to sleep upon thy billow,
    And let thy waters be my grave.

Cradle Song

SLEEP on, my poor child, sleep;
    Why must thou wake again?
Thou are but born into a world of woe,
    Of agony unending, deep,
    Of long-protracted pain.

A faint light is thrown on thine eyes,
    Alas! thy right to joy is plain:
I see thou dream'st of Paradise,
    And thou wilt only wake to pain.
    Why must thou wake again?

Wert thou not born with tears and travail?
    Thy first cry was a wail;
Life is a mystery, strange and sad,
    A wondrous riddle to unravel,
    But who shall lift the vail?

Sleep on, my poor child, sleep,
    Naught is so sweet as sleep;
Not all the joys of love,
    The tears that lovers weep;
Amber and coral from the deep,
Are not so sweet as sleep.

"Sleep on, my poor child, sleep;
    Sleep on," the mother said,
"I will sit here and weep."
    She looked on her child, asleep,
And saw the child was dead:
"'Tis well," the mother said.

Child Grief

WOULD you ask of weeping children
    A reason why they cry?
They weep, they cannot help it,
   They cannot tell you why.

Perhaps they have some forecast
   Of strange unknown desire,
That burns their dawning spirits
   With dim, uncertain fire.

Perhaps they have felt some echo,
   Of the world's unending woes,
The everlasting struggle,
   Of tyrants and of foes.

Perhaps they have some remembrance
   Of brighter, bygone things,

The music of angels' voices,
    The rustling of angels' wings—

Some faint and weird remembrance
    Of faces bright and fair,
And see but the spirit of evil,
    Who reigneth everywhere.

Ye dwellers in the valley,
    Where is that mystic hill,
That the dying see already,
    And the child rememb'reth still?

The Two Sleepers and One that Watcheth

Question.

TWO that sleep, and one that waketh,
    Biding the coming of the day,
Till the glorious morning breaketh,
    And the shadows flee away.

When the glorious morn be broken,
    And the shadows fled away,
Shall then the other twain be woken,
    To greet the dawning of the day?

Answer.

PERHAPS the day will never break,
    Nor the dark shadows flee away,
'Tis hardly worth our while to wake,
    Biding the coming of the day.

To sleep is better than to wake,
    To die is better than to sleep;
Perhaps the day will never break,
    'Tis not worth while our watch to keep.

Παιδικά

OH, Ganymede, give me the goblet
    Of golden, sparkling wine,
Yea, even if poison be in it,
    I will take from those hands of thine.

I drink of the light of thine eyes,
    In long-drawn sensual sips,
Of thy bosom's infinite warmth,
    Of the panting breath of thy lips.

I am wholly intoxicated
    As I gaze on that sweet, soft face,
Thy cheeks are pomegranates cleaving,
    Thy lips are as scarlet lace.

Thou art fairer than woman, and warmer,
    As the sun is more warm than the moon;

Thou art fairer than woman, and softer,
    As the dawn is more soft than the noon.

Oh, give me to drink, for nothing
    My thirst can satiate;
I drink, I have drunk and am drunken,
    I am wholly inebriate.

Ζιζάνια

ONCE we were bound with one another,
    Bound by an everlasting band,
Thou wert to me far more than brother,
   And infinitely more than friend.

The world may think that bond is broken,
   The world may think so, it is well;
I have one lock of hair, as token
   That it will be renewed in Hell.

∽

I am guilty before thee, I ask not for pardon,
   For my sin is endlessly great;
I am punished enough, for the love once
       between us
   Is slowly corroding to hate.

With Cain I will say, the deserved retribution
    Is harder than I can bear;
Unshriven I live, I die unrepenting,
    In terrible, utter despair.

༄

Remember me in after years,
    Who loved thee long ago;
Thou wilt find none more fond, I think,
    In this bitter world of woe.

And if some maiden beautiful
    Become thy love and joy,
Think on that passionate male heart
    That loved thee when a boy.

A thousand arrows pierce my heart,
    To see another sit beside thee;
A keener and a fiercer dart
    Pierces my soul when others chide thee.

I think I could not have the heart
    To speak thee harshly or reprove thee;
Heartless and less and worthless as thou art,
    I cannot otherwise than love thee.

All Souls' Day

COME, let us bring some flowers for the dead
Not many tears on their cold tombs are shed;
Now, in this last sad season of the year,
Let us remember those we once held dear.
Now that the leaves are scattered from the trees,
And the wild wind sighs round the tombs of these;
If they are sensible to love or hate
The dead must think the living so ingrate.

༺༻

Unto the sun I say,
    I am weary of the light,
I am weary of the day,
When shall it pass away?
    Would God that it were night.

I cry, in the dead of night,
    Would God that it were day,
I cannot sleep, I wake,
When shall the daylight break,
    And the shadows flee away?
Give me, oh, give me light!

Sapphics

THE silver stars quiver no more in the liquid
        heaven;
The waste white moon is covered with the tresses
        of midnight;
The hour of love is passed and over,
    I lie alone here.

As the hart panteth for the brooks at mid-day,
So my soul panteth for thy soft embraces;
Lying alone at the desolate hour of midnight,
    Sleepless and weary.

༄

Give me water for my head,
    And a fountain of tears for mine eyes,
A fountain of tears to shed,

  To soften the hot, dry sighs
Of my stricken spirit that weeps
  For the life of my life that is dead,
Or is not dead but sleeps—
'Tis a weary thing," she said.

     ❧

Entwined in thy limbs I lie, my love,
  Abide with me but for a little space;
How happy should I be to die, my love,
  Under thy saving kiss, in thy embrace.

Would that my life's short span were passed,
   my love;
  If the gods granted prayers then I would pray—
One long full kiss, the very last, my love,
  And then to sleep, for ever and for aye.

Translations from Heine

THOU hast both diamonds and pearls,
    Hast all to what man can aspire,
Thou hast the most beautiful eyes—
    My love, what more can'st thou desire?

I have written immortal songs,
    To sing them I never shall tire,
On thy most beautiful eyes—
    My love, what more can'st thou desire?

With thy most beautiful eyes
    Thou has burnt me through as with fire,
Thou hast wasted my soul away,
    My love, what more can'st thou desire?

It is an old, old story,
    So often told again,
And whom it lightly touches,
    His heart it rends in twain.

I DREAMED of you, my love,
    I dreamed that you were dead;
A sad but not bitter tear,
    As I waked from my dream, I shed.

I dreamed of you, my love,
    That you had deserted me;
As I waked from my dream I wept
    Long, and very bitterly.

I dreamed of you, my love,
    That you were still good and true;
I hardly ceased to weep,
    My love, as I thought of you.

SILENTLY, swiftly the rider rode
    By the echoing mountain cave:
"Do I go to the arms of my beloved,
    Or to the cold, dark grave?"
And the echo answer gave:
"To the cold, dark grave."

Further, further the rider rode
    By the echoing mountain cave:
"What! shall I die so young, so young?
    Ah well! there is rest in the grave."
And the echo answer gave:
"Rest in the grave."

The rider almost wept as he passed
    By the echoing mountain cave:

"If in the grave there is rest for me,
    I deem 'tis well in the grave."
And the echo answer gave:
"Well in the grave."

"Ganymede" from Goethe

AS in the light of the morning
Thou shinest round about me,
   Spring beloved—
   The intense feeling
   Of thy endless warmth
Presses me even unto the heart
With thousandfold delights of love,
   Infinite beauty.

Ah! that I might embrace thee
   In this arm.

I lie on thy bosom and languish,
And thy flowers, thy grass,
   Press on my heart—
Thou coolest the burning
Thirst of my bosom,

Lovely wind of the morning;
    The nightingale calls,
    Loving unto me;

From the valley of the shadow
    I come—I come,
    Where? Ah where?

    Upwards—upwards
    The clouds part, and float
    Downwards, the clouds
Yield before love's desire
    To me—to me,
    In thy bosom,
        Upwards
    Embracing, embraced
Upwards to thy bosom
    All-loving Father.

Dedication

To My Unknown Ideal

THESE wild effusions of a stricken soul,
    Life of my life, I dedicate to thee.

I think I saw thee bodily but once,
Yet in my spirit ever, and sometimes
Embodied in the vision of a dream:—

Strange sounds of strange and moving melody,
The passion of the viol's quivering string,
The high sublimity of organ tones,
    Remind me of thee strangely.

I almost think I knew thee long ago,
When present was not present, past not past,
And in a multitude of earthly forms
    I sought to see thy beauty visible.

All that is beautiful upon the earth
    Is but an image, though so faint, of thee.
Lo, I have sought thee—I have not found thee.

A PARTIAL LIST OF SNUGGLY BOOKS

LÉON BLOY *The Tarantulas' Parlor and Other Unkind Tales*
S. HENRY BERTHOUD *Misanthropic Tales*
JAMES CHAMPAGNE *Harlem Smoke*
FÉLICIEN CHAMPSAUR *The Latin Orgy*
FÉLICIEN CHAMPSAUR
   The Emerald Princess and Other Decadent Fantasies
BRENDAN CONNELL *Clark*
BRENDAN CONNELL *Unofficial History of Pi Wei*
ADOLFO COUVE *When I Think of My Missing Head*
QUENTIN S. CRISP *Aiaigasa*
QUENTIN S. CRISP *Graves*
LADY DILKE *The Outcast Spirit and Other Stories*
CATHERINE DOUSTEYSSIER-KHOZE
   The Beauty of the Death Cap
BERIT ELLINGSEN *Now We Can See the Moon*
BERIT ELLINGSEN *Vessel and Solsvart*
EDMOND AND JULES DE GONCOURT *Manette Salomon*
GUIDO GOZZANO *Alcina and Other Stories*
RHYS HUGHES *Cloud Farming in Wales*
J.-K. HUYSMANS *Knapsacks*
COLIN INSOLE *Valerie and Other Stories*
JUSTIN ISIS *Pleasant Tales II*
JUSTIN ISIS (editor) *Marked to Die: A Tribute to Mark Samuels*
JUSTIN ISIS AND DANIEL CORRICK (editors)
   Drowning in Beauty: The Neo-Decadent Anthology
VICTOR JOLY
   The Unknown Collaborator and Other Legendary Tales

BERNARD LAZARE *The Mirror of Legends*
BERNARD LAZARE *The Torch-Bearers*
MAURICE LEVEL *The Shadow*
JEAN LORRAIN *Errant Vice*
JEAN LORRAIN *Masks in the Tapestry*
JEAN LORRAIN *Nightmares of an Ether-Drinker*
JEAN LORRAIN
    The Soul-Drinker and Other Decadent Fantasies
ARTHUR MACHEN *N*
ARTHUR MACHEN *Ornaments in Jade*
CAMILLE MAUCLAIR *The Frail Soul and Other Stories*
CATULLE MENDÈS *Bluebirds*
CATULLE MENDÈS *Mephistophela*
ÉPHRAÏM MIKHAËL *Halyartes and Other Poems in Prose*
LUIS DE MIRANDA *Who Killed the Poet?*
OCTAVE MIRBEAU *The Death of Balzac*
TERESA WILMS MONTT *In the Stillness of Marble*
CHARLES MORICE *Babels, Balloons and Innocent Eyes*
DAMIAN MURPHY *Daughters of Apostasy*
DAMIAN MURPHY *The Star of Gnosia*
KRISTINE ONG MUSLIM *Butterfly Dream*
YARROW PAISLEY *Mendicant City*
URSULA PFLUG *Down From*
ADOLPHE RETTÉ *Misty Thule*
JEAN RICHEPIN *The Bull-Man and the Grasshopper*
DAVID RIX *A Suite in Four Windows*
FREDERICK ROLFE (Baron Corvo) *Amico di Sandro*
FREDERICK ROLFE (Baron Corvo)
    An Ossuary of the North Lagoon and Other Stories
JASON ROLFE *An Archive of Human Nonsense*

BRIAN STABLEFORD (editor)
Decadence and Symbolism: A Showcase Anthology
BRIAN STABLEFORD *The Insubstantial Pageant*
BRIAN STABLEFORD *Spirits of the Vasty Deep*
COUNT ERIC STENBOCK *Myrtle, Rue and Cypress*
COUNT ERIC STENBOCK *The Shadow of Death*
COUNT ERIC STENBOCK *Studies of Death*
DOUGLAS THOMPSON *The Fallen West*
TOADHOUSE *Gone Fishing with Samy Rosenstock*
JANE DE LA VAUDÈRE *The Demi-Sexes and The Androgynes*
JANE DE LA VAUDÈRE
The Double Star and Other Occult Fantasies
JANE DE LA VAUDÈRE
The Mystery of Kama and Brahma's Courtesans
RENÉE VIVIEN *Lilith's Legacy*
RENÉE VIVIEN *A Woman Appeared to Me*
RENÉE VIVIEN AND HÉLÈNE DE ZUYLEN DE NYEVELT
Faustina and Other Stories
KAREL VAN DE WOESTIJNE *The Dying Peasant*

www.ingramcontent.com/pod-product-compliance
Lightning Source LLC
Chambersburg PA
CBHW020128130526
44591CB00032B/568